The Big Book of Primary Physical Science

Motion, Magnets and More

Compiled from the following books:
Move It! © 2005
Touch It! © 2005
Build It! © 2006
Change It! © 2006

Kids Can Press acknowledges the financial support of the Government of Ontario, through the Ontario Media Development Corporation's Ontario Book Initiative; the Ontario Arts Council; the Canada Council for the Arts; and the Government of Canada, through the BPIDP, for our publishing activity.

Published in Canada by
Kids Can Press Ltd.
25 Dockside Drive
Toronto, ON M5A 0B5

Published in the U.S. by
Kids Can Press Ltd.
2250 Military Road
Tonawanda, NY 14150

www.kidscanpress.com

Edited by Valerie Wyatt
Designed by Julia Naimska

This book is smyth sewn casebound.
Manufactured in Shenzhen, China, in 4/2011 through Asia Pacific Offset

CM 11 0 9 8 7 6 5 4 3 2 1

Library and Archives Canada Cataloguing in Publication

Mason, Adrienne
     Motion, magnets and more : the big book of primary physical science / written by Adrienne Mason ; illustrated by Claudia Dávila.

Includes the original separately published texts of: Build it!, Change it!, Move it!,
     and Touch it!.

ISBN 978-1-55453-707-5

     1. Physical sciences—Juvenile literature. I. Dávila, Claudia II. Title.

Q163.M375 2011   j500.2   C2011-901074-7

Kids Can Press is a **forus**™ Entertainment company

The Big Book of Primary Physical Science

Motion, Magnets and More

Written by **Adrienne Mason**
Illustrated by **Claudia Dávila**

Kids Can Press

Contents

Touch It!

Materials, matter and you

A material world

Stone, metal, paper, plastic — these are different materials. Everything around you is made of some kind of material. A marble is made of glass, and this book is made of paper.

How many different materials can you see in the picture?

Material mosaic

Use different materials to make a mosaic picture.

You will need

- small objects made of different materials, such as stones, buttons, coins, beads, shells, pasta or seeds
- a muffin tin
- white glue
- a small piece of cardboard

What to do

1 Sort your objects into groups of the same material. You might have one group of stones, another of plastic objects and another of metal, for example. Use one muffin cup for each group.

2 Make a mosaic picture by gluing the objects to the cardboard.

What's happening?

Your picture is made of objects made from different materials. Some objects, such as a wood button, are made of one material. Other objects, such as pasta, are made of more than one material.

This tricycle is made of many different materials.

Describing materials

Different materials have different shapes, colors and sizes. A plum is round, purple and small. A banana is long, yellow and bigger than a plum. You can use your senses of sight, touch, smell and even taste to describe materials.

How would you compare a strawberry and a pineapple?

Touchy materials

Different materials have different textures. Texture is the way something feels when you touch it. A rabbit's fur feels soft. A wood fence feels hard. Soft, hard, rough, smooth and prickly all describe textures.

What kinds of textures do the objects and creatures in this farmyard have?

How does it feel?

What are different textures used for? Try this guessing activity.

You will need
- a scarf
- several objects made of materials with different textures, such as a paper towel, bath towel, baking pan, piece of paper, sandpaper, hairbrush and ball of wool

What to do

1 Tie the scarf around a friend's eyes so she can't see.

2 Hand your friend different objects to touch. Have her describe the texture of each one.

3 Ask your friend to guess what each object might be used for.

What's happening?
Materials with different textures have different uses. A smooth piece of paper is good for writing on. Rough sandpaper helps to polish wood.

Mass of materials

All materials, like these vegetables, have mass. Mass is the amount of stuff in an object. An object's mass can change when its size changes. As you grow, your mass will increase.

In the picture, which dog has more mass?

Comparing mass

Do objects of the same size, such as a coin and a button, have the same mass? Try this activity to find out.

You will need

- an eraser
- a ruler
- 2 paper drinking cups
- a coin
- a plastic button the same size as the coin

What to do

1 Place the eraser on its side. Balance the ruler on the eraser.

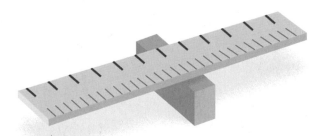

2 Put a paper cup on either end of the ruler. You have made a simple scale.

3 Place the coin in one cup and the button in the other. What happens?

4 Which has more mass, the metal coin or the plastic button? How do you know?

What's happening?

On your scale, the cup containing more mass will dip lower. Objects that are the same size but made of different materials often have a different mass.

This bowling ball has more mass than the soccer ball.

Floating materials

When a leaf falls onto a pond, it floats. But if you throw a stone, it sinks. Some materials float, while others sink.

The shape of an object can make a difference. A ball of clay will sink. But if you shape it into a boat, it will float.

Magnetic materials

You can use a magnet to attach a picture to your fridge, but not to a window or a table. Why not?

Some materials are magnetic. The kind of metal in this fridge door is magnetic, but glass and wood are not. Magnets attract magnetic materials. They pull toward one another.

Magnetic attraction

Which materials are magnetic? Find out with this activity.

You will need
- a magnet
- a number of small objects, such as a paper clip, key, marble, coin, eraser, nail, crayon, cork and stone

What to do

1 Without using the magnet, try sorting your objects into two groups — magnetic and not magnetic.

2 Now use the magnet to test all of the objects. Did you sort them into the correct groups? Which ones are magnetic?

What's happening?
Only objects made of metal materials are magnetic. Many types of metal are magnetic, but some metals are not. Objects made of other materials, such as plastic and glass, are not magnetic.

Using materials

Certain materials are used to make certain objects. Glass is a good material for windows. It is clear, so you can see through it. Metal, cloth and rubber are useful for other things.

   Look at this picture. What are the objects made of? Why are those materials good for these objects?

Stretchy materials

Do some materials stretch more than others?

You will need

- one strip each of plastic wrap, newspaper, plastic grocery bag, paper towel and waxed paper, about 2 cm x 20 cm (1 in. x 8 in.)

What to do

1 Hold one end of the strip of plastic wrap firmly. Have your friend hold onto the other end.

2 Pull on the ends. What happens?

3 Try pulling on the other materials. Which material stretches most? Why do you think it needs to stretch?

What's happening?

Some materials are stretchier than others. Plastic wrap is stretchy so that it can be used to seal food tightly in containers. Newspaper, paper towels and waxed paper do not have to be as stretchy because they have different uses.

The material in my web is strong and stretchy — good for catching insects.

Materials around us

Objects are made of different materials.
Certain materials are better for certain uses.

Some materials float.

Some materials stretch.

Some materials are hard.

Some materials are soft.

33

Build It!

Structures, systems and you

Structures around you

Structures are objects that are made of parts. This wooden bench is a structure. Its parts are the seat, back, arms and legs. These parts are joined together with nails and screws.

Bicycles and jackets are structures, too. Can you find five more structures in this picture?

It's natural!

People build structures and so do some animals. A bird builds its nest from grass and twigs. A beaver makes its dam from tree trunks and branches.

In this picture, can you find three more structures built by animals?

Build it!

Can you build a structure using food?

You will need
- square crackers
- a butter knife
- peanut butter or cream cheese
- toothpicks
- ju-jubes or marshmallows
- dry lasagna noodles

What to do

1 Decide which materials you want to use as the parts of your structure. Which could you use to join the parts?

2 Combine two or more materials to make a structure. For example, spread a thin layer of peanut butter or cream cheese on the edges of 6 crackers. Then join them to make a box.

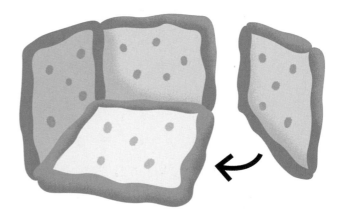

3 Make other structures, such as a house or a bridge. What other food items could you use?

What's happening?

You can combine different objects to make structures. In this activity, the parts of the structures are types of food.

Maybe I can use this structure to find a snack.

What's it for?

A tent and a doghouse are structures made with different materials. A tent is made with lightweight poles and fabric so it can be carried around. A doghouse is made with pieces of wood — it is built to stay in one place.

In this picture, how are the two umbrellas different?

Staying together

You can join the parts of structures in many ways. Nails join pieces of wood together. A zipper holds the two sides of a jacket together.

In this picture, can you see other ways to join parts together?

Join it!

Try joining parts to make a structure — a puppet!

You will need

- a pencil
- poster board
- scissors
- tape
- 2 drinking straws or chopsticks
- a hole punch
- a paper fastener

What to do

1 Draw a side view of a bird without a wing. Cut it out.

2 Draw a bird wing and cut it out. Tape 1 straw to the back of the wing.

3 Punch a hole through the wing and the bird body. Put a paper fastener through the holes.

4 Tape the other straw to the back of the bird's body.

5 Make your puppet move and flap its wing.

What's happening?
You used the paper fastener and tape to join the parts of your puppet.

My backpack is a structure. Its parts are joined with thread, zippers and buckles.

Layer it!

You can make a structure by using layers.
The parts of a piñata are layers of paper
and paste. The more layers a piñata has,
the harder it is to break open.

Can you find other structures with layers?
Why do you think they have layers?

Tough tissues

A tissue is a structure made of layers. What do the layers do? Try this to find out.

You will need

- 2 pieces of facial tissue
- an empty plastic container, such as a margarine tub
- an elastic band
- 100 pennies

What to do

1 A tissue is made of two or three layers. Take one tissue and carefully pull apart the layers.

2 Place one layer of the tissue over the container. Ask an adult to use the elastic band to hold the layer in place.

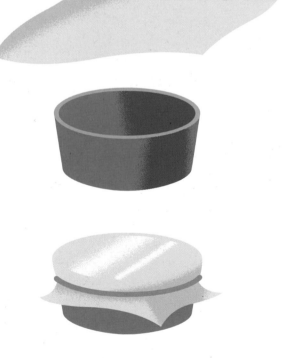

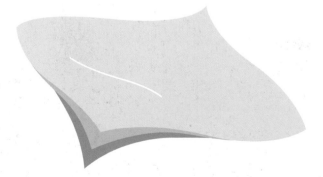

3 Hold your hand about 10 cm (4 in.) above the tissue. Drop pennies, one at a time, until the layer tears. How many pennies fell into the container?

What's happening?

The second tissue was stronger because it had two (or three) layers. Strong tissues are important when you have to sneeze.

4 Take the second tissue, but do not separate the layers. Repeat steps 2 and 3. Do layers make the tissue stronger?

Layers of paper, plastic and foil make my juice box strong.

Twist and fold

Twisting and folding can make a structure more useful. You can make a rope thicker and stronger by twisting two ropes together. A sheet of paper is floppy. By folding it, you can make it stiff. Now you can use it as a fan.

Fold it!

Does folding make a structure stronger? Try this to find out.

You will need

- a 10 cm x 20 cm (4 in. x 8 in.) strip of paper
- 2 plastic glasses or small containers
- 20 pennies

What to do

1 Place the paper strip across the glasses to form a bridge.

2 Place a few pennies on the bridge. Did your bridge collapse?

3 Fold the paper back and forth along the long edge.

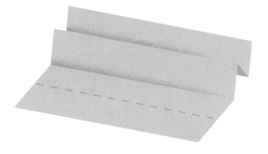

4 Place the folded paper strip across the glasses.

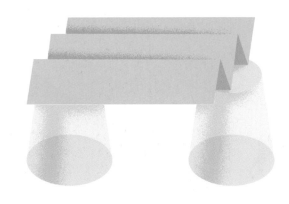

54

5 Place pennies on the bridge again. Can you add more pennies now?

What's happening?

By folding the paper, you changed the bridge and made this structure stronger.

Three layers, with the middle layer folded, make cardboard really strong.

Strong shapes

Some shapes make structures stronger.
Arches and domes are both strong shapes.
The palace doorway is an arch. The igloo
is a dome. Why do you think these
structures need to be strong?

Can you see another dome and other
arches in the picture?

Triangle power

A triangle shape can make a structure stronger. How? Try this to find out.

You will need

- twelve short 5 cm (2 in.) pieces of dry spaghetti
- 8 mini-marshmallows
- a playing card
- 20 pennies
- four long 7 cm (3 in.) pieces of dry spaghetti

What to do

1 Make a box using the short pieces of spaghetti and the mini-marshmallows.

2 Place the playing card on top of the box. Pile pennies on the card, one at a time, until the box collapses.

3 Add one long piece of spaghetti across each side of the box as shown. This makes triangle shapes.

4 Repeat step two. Now how many pennies can you pile on before the box collapses?

What's happening?

Triangles don't shift or twist as easily as squares or rectangles do. This makes triangles useful in structures that need to be strong.

These spokes make triangles that keep my wheels strong.

Get building!

A structure is an object or building made of parts joined together.

Parts are joined in different ways.

Parts can be changed to make structures stronger.

Triangles, arches and domes make structures stronger.

Change It!
Solids, liquids, gases and you

Matter around you

Matter is all around you. You are matter, a toy boat is matter and water is matter. Matter is anything that takes up space. Matter can be a solid, a liquid or a gas.

What's a solid?

Solids have their own shape. Rocks are solids. Hats and skipping ropes are solids, too. Solids don't change shape easily. You can stretch a skipping rope, but when you let it go it takes its own shape again.

Can you find three more solid objects in the picture?

Change its shape!

Play dough is a kind of solid. If you change its shape, is it still a solid? Make some and see.

You will need

- 250 mL (1 cup) flour
- 60 mL (1/4 cup) salt
- a mixing bowl
- a spoon
- 125 mL (1/2 cup) hot tap water
- food coloring

What to do

1 Mix the flour and salt in the bowl.

2 Have an adult add the hot water. Stir well.

3 Use your hands to knead the dough. If it is too sticky, add a sprinkle of flour.

5 Use the dough to make different shapes. Store leftover dough in a plastic container in the fridge.

4 Add the food coloring and knead for 5 minutes.

What's happening?

The play dough keeps the shape you mold it into. Solids keep their shape unless you do something to change them.

I changed the shape of this chocolate bar, but both parts are still solid.

What's a liquid?

A liquid has no shape of its own. Liquids change shape easily. Liquids also flow. When you pour a liquid into a container, it takes the shape of the container — a glass, a bottle or a bucket.

How many liquids can you find in this picture?

Pour it in!

Can your friend guess which container holds more liquid? Find out.

You will need

- a measuring cup
- water
- 3 empty clear plastic or glass containers of different sizes and shapes
- food coloring

What to do

1 When your friend isn't watching, pour 250 mL (1 cup) of water into each container.

2 Add two drops of food coloring to each container.

3 Ask your friend to guess which container holds the most water.

4 Pour the water from the container your friend chose back into the measuring cup. Show her how much water was in the container.

5 Now pour the water from the other containers into the measuring cup, one at a time. Your friend will see that each container was holding the same amount of liquid.

What's happening?
Liquids take the shape of their containers. The amount of liquid can look greater or smaller depending on the container.

Uh-oh! This container is too small.

What's a gas?

Gas is all around you, even if you can't see it.
The air you breathe in and blow out is a gas.
A gas has no shape of its own. Gases
spread out to fill their container — a bubble,
a bicycle tire or even a room.

Fill it up!

Can you fill a balloon without blowing air into it?
Try this.

You will need

- a balloon
- a small funnel
- a teaspoon
- baking soda
- vinegar
- a juice or pop bottle

What to do

1 Stretch the neck of the balloon.

2 Put the funnel into the neck of the balloon. Add two large spoonfuls of baking soda to the balloon.

3 Pour vinegar into the bottle. Stop when it is half full.

4 Ask an adult to help you with this step. Stretch the neck of the balloon over the opening of the bottle.

5 Hold the balloon upright. Let the baking soda fall into the vinegar.

What's happening?

When you combine baking soda and vinegar, they make a gas. This gas spreads out to fill the bottle and then the balloon.

The fizz in my pop comes from tiny bubbles of gas.

Freezing and melting

Solids can change into liquids when they warm up. When a solid snowflake lands on your warm tongue, it melts and changes into liquid water.

Liquids can change into solids when they cool down. Because it's cold out, the water in this pond has frozen into ice.

Cool it!

How can liquids and solids combine to make ice cream? Try this to find out.

You will need
- 250 mL (1 cup) whole milk (a liquid)
- 5 mL (1 teaspoon) vanilla (a liquid)
- 15 mL (1 tablespoon) sugar (a solid)
- 1 small sealable plastic bag
- 1 large sealable plastic bag
- 12 ice cubes (solids)
- 30 mL (2 tablespoons) salt (a solid)

What to do

1 Put the milk, vanilla and sugar into the small plastic bag. Seal the bag well.

2 Place the ice cubes in the large plastic bag. Sprinkle the salt on the ice.

3 Place the small bag in the large bag. Seal the large bag well.

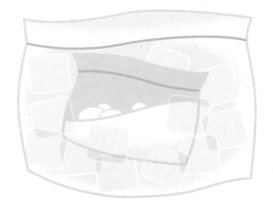

4 Put on some music and shake the bag for 10 minutes.

5 Scoop your ice cream into a bowl and enjoy.

What's happening?

The ice cools the milk and sugar. Then this liquid mixture changes into a solid — ice cream.

I'd better eat my ice cream fast before it melts into a liquid.

Wonderful water

After it rains, there are puddles. But puddles soon dry up. The warmth of the sun makes liquid water change into a gas. This gas is called "water vapor."

Water can be a liquid, a solid or a gas. Can you find all three in this picture?

82

Paint with salt!

How can you make a picture by painting with salty water? Try this to find out.

You will need

- 60 mL (1/4 cup) warm water
- a small plastic or glass container
- 30 mL (2 tablespoons) Epsom salts
- a paintbrush
- 1 piece dark construction paper

2 With the paintbrush, paint a simple picture on the construction paper.

What to do

1 Pour the warm water into the container. Add the salt. Use the paintbrush to mix the salt in the water.

3 Let the paper dry. What do you see? Where did the water go?

What's happening?

The warm water disappears because it changes into water vapor. The salt, a solid, stays on the paper and makes your picture.

High in the sky, water vapor cools down and turns into clouds.

Mixing matter

You can combine solids and liquids to make something new. When you bake a cake, you mix together eggs and milk (liquids) with flour, sugar and butter (solids). When you put the mixture into a hot oven, gas bubbles form. This gas makes the batter rise so you get a fluffy cake.

Solids, liquids and gases

Matter is anything that takes up space. Matter can be a solid, a liquid or a gas.

Solids don't change shape easily. They have to be pushed or pulled, heated or cooled.

Liquids can flow. They take the shape of the container they are in.

Gases have no shape. They spread out to fill the space they are in.

Move It!

Motion, forces and you

Push and pull

You use pushes and pulls to make things move. A push moves an object away. A pull brings it closer. A push or a pull is called a force.

Move it!

You use force to move your body. To walk, you push against the ground. You also use force to move things. You pull a wagon to make it move.

Can you find five ways these children are using force to move their bodies or other things?

Push it!

It takes force to move things. Does it take more force to move heavy things? Try this to find out.

You will need
- 3 identical, opaque plastic tubs with lids
- small rocks or marbles
- uncooked macaroni or other small pasta
- crumpled paper

What to do

1 Fill one tub with rocks or marbles, one with pasta and one with crumpled paper.

2 Put the lids on the tubs. Ask a helper to move the tubs around until you don't know which is which.

3 Push each tub across the table. Which tub took the most force (the biggest push) to move? What do you think is in it? Which took the least force (the smallest push) to move? What do you think is in it? Remove the lids to see if you were right.

What's happening?

It takes more force (a bigger push) to move heavy things, like the rocks. It takes less force (a smaller push) to move lighter things.

Make it move

Things do not move unless they are pushed or pulled. When you lift something, you are pulling it up. When you throw something, you are pushing it away.

Can you find five ways these children are using pushes or pulls to make things move?

Go the distance

To throw a ball to someone far away, you need to use a lot of force (a big push). To throw to someone closer, you need less force. The more force you use to move something, the greater the distance it will move.

Puffing power

Does a big force make things move faster?
Try this to find out.

You will need

- a Ping-Pong ball
- a drinking straw

What to do

1 Place the Ping-Pong ball on a table.

2 Move the ball by blowing through the straw at it.

3 Blow softly. What happens? Blow harder. Does the ball go faster or slower?

4 Have a race with a friend to see who can make their ball go fastest.

What's happening?

When you use a small force (blow lightly), the ball moves slowly. When you use a bigger force (blow harder), the ball moves faster.

The more force I use to push against the water, the faster I move.

Move it on over

When you kick a ball it moves in a straight line, unless it is then kicked from the side. All things move in a straight line unless they are pushed or pulled from a different direction. A kick is just a push with your foot.

Stop it!

To stop something that is moving, you need to use force. You stop a ball by pushing in the opposite direction.

The faster something moves, the more force it takes to stop it.

Down to Earth

If you throw something up, it will fall back down. It is pulled down by a force called gravity.

You can't see gravity, but it pulls things — including you — down toward Earth. This is why things fall to the ground when you drop them.

Lift it!

It takes force to overcome gravity and lift things. Does it take more force to lift heavy things?

You will need

- a small nail
- a small, empty yogurt tub
- three 15 cm (6 in.) long pieces of string
- a rubber band
- marbles or small rocks
- a ruler

What to do

1 Have an adult use the nail to make three evenly spaced holes around the rim of the plastic tub.

2 Thread one piece of string through each hole and tie a knot to hold the end in place.

3 Tie the free ends of the string together. Slip the rubber band through the knotted end as shown.

110

4 Put the tub on the floor and add one marble. Hold the elastic band by the end and pull up until the plastic tub lifts off the floor. Measure the length of the elastic.

5 Add 5 marbles to the tub and repeat step 4. Does the length of the elastic change when there are more objects in the tub?

What's happening?

The force of gravity pulls down on the tub. You need to pull up against gravity to lift the tub. The marbles make the tub heavier, and it takes more force (a bigger pull) to lift it.

The more force you use to lift the tub, the longer the elastic band stretches.

Slow motion

You push on the pedals to make your bicycle move. When you stop pushing, your bicycle slows down and stops. Why?

Your bicycle tires are rubbing against the road. When two surfaces rub together there is a force called friction.

Friction makes moving things slow down and then stop. Friction also helps you grip the ground when you walk or run.

Sliding along

Friction happens when things rub together. Is friction always the same? Try this to find out.

You will need

- a bread board
- an eraser
- a small stone
- a small wooden block
- an ice cube

What to do

1 Put the bread board on a table. Line up the eraser, stone, block and ice cube at one end of the board.

2 Carefully lift the end of the board until one object begins to slide. Lift more and watch how fast the objects slide. Do some slide faster than others? Why do you think this is?

3 Try other small objects you find around the house. Which one slides best?

What's happening?

There is more friction between some materials than others. With the rubber eraser the friction is greater. With the ice cube the friction is less.

There is not much friction between my smooth shell and the snow.

Get moving!

A force is a push or a pull that starts an object moving or changes its motion.

A force can start an object moving.

A force can stop a moving object.

A force can change the direction
of an object that is already moving.

For parents and teachers

The information and activities in this book are designed to teach children about the physical sciences. Here are some ways you can explore the concepts further.

Touch It!

A material world, pages 8–9
Ask children to look for places where the same type of material has different uses. For example, glass can be used in windows, in drinking glasses or in eyeglasses. Explain the difference between objects and materials. A cup is an object; it can be made of materials such as porcelain, glass, paper or plastic.

Material mosaic, pages 10–11
Have children look for objects that are made of one material (e.g., a drinking glass) and those made of several different materials (e.g., toys made with metal and plastic). They could sort the objects they collect for the activity in this way as well. Pasta, for example, is made of two materials — flour and water.

Describing materials, pages 12–13
Shape, color and size are properties of materials. Have children sort and describe objects using words for shape, color and size. Encourage them to use their senses of sight, touch and smell to describe materials, but make sure "taste" is used only for foods. Hearing can be used also: lightly tap a pencil against metal, glass, ceramic, wood and plastic objects and have children describe the sounds.

Touchy materials, pages 14–15
Texture is a property of materials. Ask children to find objects with many different textures. Encourage them to compare the textures of similar objects and discuss how texture relates to each object's use. For example, why do running shoes or hiking boots have rough soles, while dancing shoes have smooth soles?

How does it feel?, pages 16–17
Discuss how the texture of an object gives a clue as to how it might be used. For example, the rough texture of a paper towel suggests that it would be better for absorbing liquid than the smooth texture of a sheet of writing paper.

Mass of materials, pages 18–19
Mass is a property of materials. The mass of an object is how much matter it contains. An object's mass is always the same, regardless of where it is in the universe. In contrast, weight is a measure of the force of gravity acting upon an object. So weight varies according to where in the universe an object is. At this age, children don't need to know the difference between mass and weight, but be sure they use the correct term — mass — when comparing objects.

Comparing mass, pages 20–21
Have ready a variety of objects that are the same size but made of different materials. Ask children to compare their mass. They will discover that objects may be the same size, but if they are made of different materials their mass may vary.

Floating materials, pages 22–23
Buoyancy is a property of materials. Demonstrate how changing the shape of an object can sometimes change its buoyancy. Put a lump of clay in a bowl of water and watch it sink. Then shape it into a boat and watch it float. Children could test the buoyancy of similarly-sized objects made of different materials. For example, cut a piece of cardboard to the same size as a coin and try to float both objects.

Magnetic materials and **Magnetic attraction,** pages 24–27
Magnetism is a property of materials. Magnets attract objects made of the metals iron, nickel and cobalt. A magnet will pick up objects such as pins, nails and paper clips because they are made of steel, which contains iron. Children could use magnets to find magnetic and non-magnetic materials in the classroom or at home. Keep magnets away from computers and cards with magnetic stripes.

Using materials, pages 28–29
Have children sort objects into groups and see what materials are used for these objects. In a classroom, scissors, pencils, crayons, erasers, paper and other school supplies could be sorted. What kinds of materials are used in each type of object? Why are certain materials better for certain uses? For example, why are scissors made of metal and not wood?

Stretchy materials, pages 30–31
Flexibility is a property of materials. Some materials stretch farther before they tear or snap. Plastics are made of molecules that are strong and stretch quite a bit before they break. Papers are made of fibers that are not as strong. Have children describe the uses of objects that are made of stretchy materials such as plastic wrap, rubber, elastic and stretchy fabrics.

Materials around us, pages 32–33
Buoyancy, stretchiness and hardness are properties of materials. Size, color, shape, texture, transparency, mass and magnetic attraction are also properties of materials. Challenge children to choose one object and describe at least three different properties of the materials used in that object. Encourage them to use as many of their senses as they can.

Build It!

Structures around you, pages 36–37
Ask children to look for structures in the house, neighborhood or classroom. They should understand that structures are not just buildings, bridges or towers. Clothes, toys, vehicles and even plants are structures, too. Have

children think about what parts make up the structures they identify.

It's natural!, pages 38–39

Three additional animal-built structures include a wasp nest, an anthill and a spiderweb. Ask children to talk about the parts of animal-built structures. For example, an anthill may be built from sand or pine needles and a wasp nest from bits of wood mixed with saliva. Children could also examine other natural structures, such as a feather and a cocoon.

Build it!, pages 40–41

Have children explore ways of building structures. Cream cheese, peanut butter, ju-jubes and marshmallows can all be used to join crackers or lasagna noodles. There is no right or wrong way to build the structures, although different methods will affect the stability, strength and function of the structure. Other useful food items include dry spaghetti and fresh peas.

What's it for?, pages 42–43

Structures are made for different purposes, and purpose affects the materials chosen. Eagles use sticks to build large nests, while hummingbirds use grass, moss and spiderwebs for their tiny ones. People use cloth for umbrellas that need to last and paper for decorative umbrellas. Ask children why similar structures, such as a running shoe and a rain boot, are made of different materials.

Staying together and Join it!, pages 44–47

In this picture, parts are being joined with string, needle and thread, staples and glue, as well as nails and zippers. Have children look for other ways in which parts of structures are joined. For example, the bricks in a wall are put together with mortar. Look for hinges, screws, dowels and other kinds of fasteners used in structures.

Layer it!, pages 48–49

Layers of material, such as paper in a piñata and wood in plywood, make structures stronger, but layers can serve other purposes as well. Layers of cloth and filling make the quilt warmer, and layers joined with icing can make a cake tastier. Ask children to think about how the strength of a paper bag would change if they placed another bag inside it to make two layers.

Tough tissues, pages 50–51

Have children try this activity again using a wet tissue. How does wetness affect the strength of the tissue? Children could also place one layer of tissue on the container, then top it with a second layer turned 90 degrees. Now the grains of the two layers of tissue run in different directions. Does this change the number of pennies the layers of tissue can hold?

Twist and fold, pages 52–53

To demonstrate how twisting increases strength, plan a tug-of-war between two children. First, use two long pieces of yarn not twisted together. Then use two pieces of yarn twisted together. Which is stronger? Show that folding makes paper stronger (see the next activity) and allows children to make paper fans, hats or airplanes.

Fold it!, pages 54–55

Folding the paper makes the bridge more rigid and able to support more coins. Have children look for places where structures include parts that are folded, corrugated or pleated. For example, folds can be found in corrugated cardboard and metal, and in plastic roofing.

Strong shapes, pages 56–57

Children can find another dome on the palace roof. The bridge and the door of the igloo are arches. Domes and arches spread the weight of a structure over its base. To demonstrate the strength of a dome, put hard-boiled eggs (dome shapes) in each of the four corners of an egg carton. Place a baking sheet on top of the eggs, then pile on books, one by one. The eggs can support quite a load before cracking.

Triangle power, pages 58–59

To demonstrate that triangles are strong shapes, make both a simple rectangle and a triangle using toothpicks and marshmallows. Gently push on the two structures. Children will see that the triangle is more rigid. Ask them to look for triangle shapes in structures such as roofs, metal towers, bridges and playground equipment.

Get building!, pages 60–61

Collect a variety of structures such as toy cars, action figures, doll houses and sports equipment. Have children identify the parts of these structures and how they are joined together. Have them look at the materials used, such as rubber, metal or wood, and discuss what purpose they were chosen for. Finally, ask children to locate strong shapes — triangles, arches and domes.

Change It!

Matter around you, pages 64–65

Every living and nonliving thing is made of matter. Matter has mass and takes up space. Children will be able to understand the idea that matter is something they can see, feel or smell. There are three main states of matter: solids, liquids and gases. Ask children to identify and describe matter in the illustration and in the world around them. In the picture, the solids include the tree, boat, people and flowers. The liquid is the water in the pond. The gas is the air all around and inside the bubbles in the pond.

What's a solid?, pages 66–67

Solids have a definite mass and shape. Typical "hard" solids include metal, rocks, wood and ice. Solid matter keeps its shape unless an outside force acts upon it. A great deal of force (a push or a pull) is needed to change some solids. Other solids can change shape more easily, when only a small amount of force is applied. Collect a variety of solids for children to examine; for example, a crayon, paper clip, sponge, ribbon and cookie. Take children on a walk to look for more solids, both indoors and out.

Change its shape!, pages 68–69
Solids keep their shape unless they are pushed or pulled. Play dough is a solid whose shape can be easily changed. When children work with play dough in this activity, they can see that it holds the shape they mold it into. Talk about other ways children could change the shape of solids. For example, they can break a crayon, cut a ribbon or crumble a cookie. As with play dough, these smaller pieces hold their shape and remain solid matter.

What's a liquid? and **Pour it in!,**
pages 70–73
Liquid matter can flow. Let children experiment with a variety of liquids such as milk, liquid honey, molasses and juice. Assemble different sizes and shapes of containers. Pour the liquids from one container into another to demonstrate how they flow. For example, honey flows more slowly than milk. (Some solids, such as dry macaroni or jelly beans, can also "flow," but these small solids do not change shape after they are poured.)

What's a gas?, pages 74–75
A gas is matter that has no shape of its own. Gases spread out and fill whatever container they are in. Gases can be difficult for children to visualize. Show that they can feel a gas (moving air) when the wind blows or when they blow on their hand. To demonstrate how gases spread out to fill whatever space or container they are in, open a bag of freshly popped microwave popcorn in a room. The warm gas rising from the popcorn will fill the room. In the picture, the smell of the loaf of bread is spread by gases.

Fill it up!, pages 76–77
The balloon blows up because the gas spreads out to fill the container — the balloon. Gas pushing on the walls of the balloon inflates it. The gas produced in this reaction is carbon dioxide.

Freezing and melting and **Cool it!,**
pages 78–81
Solids and liquids can change state when they are cooled or heated. Show children some examples, such as freezing juice to make frozen treats, or melting chocolate or butter by setting it in a sunny window. Butter and chocolate will both become solid again when they are cooled in the refrigerator.

Wonderful water, pages 82–83
Water is the only substance that is found in nature as a solid, a liquid and a gas. On pages 78–79, the children saw what happens when water freezes and becomes a solid (ice). Here, they see how water can evaporate (change from a liquid to a gas). Tell children that water can also change from a gas (water vapor) to a liquid when cooled. This is called condensation. The clouds in the picture form when water

vapor cools and condenses into water droplets in the cloud.

Paint with salt!, pages 84–85
This activity demonstrates the effects of evaporation. When the water evaporates, it becomes water vapor (a gas) and leaves the salt (a solid) on the paper. Talk about other examples of evaporation, such as a wet bathing suit drying on a warm summer day.

Mixing matter, pages 86–87
Water can freeze and melt and freeze again without becoming a new kind of matter. Sometimes, however, when you change a state of matter, the process can't be reversed. In this activity, solids and liquids are mixed and then baked. The resulting solid is a different type of matter — a cake. The change is irreversible. Ask the children what happens when you cook (heat) an egg. Can this change be reversed?

Solids, liquids and gases, pages 88–89
Have children cut out pictures of the three states of matter from magazines. Make a wall chart with three columns: Solids, Liquids and Gases. Have children place their pictures in one of the three columns. For the gas column, they can show the effect of a gas; for example, a kite or flag blowing in the wind.

Move It!

Push and pull, pages 92–93
Objects are moved by pushing or pulling. When you are out for a walk or on the playground, have children describe whether various actions are pushes or pulls. Explain that when they walk, run or jump, they are pushing against the ground.

Move it!, pages 94–95
There are many ways to describe moving things, such as pushing, pulling, lifting, twirling and jumping. Put on some music and make up a dance that consists of a variety of movements. Ask children to describe all of the movements they made. Which were pushing movements and which were pulling movements?

Push it!, pages 96–97
More force (a bigger push or pull) is required to move heavier things. Test other objects and ask children to predict how much force (a little or a lot; more or less) will be needed to move them.

Make it move, pages 98–99
Things move by transferring force from one object to another. For example, when a child pushes a toy car, she is transferring force from her muscles into a pushing force on the car.

Go the distance, pages 100–101
The strength of a force applied to an object affects how far it will travel. With more force, an object travels farther. Experiment with this idea by having children use different amounts of force to kick a ball or push a toy car. Measure or note how far the ball or car travels each time.

Puffing power, pages 102–103
The strength of a force applied to an object affects how fast it will travel. With more force, an object travels faster. In a large space, have children roll a ball over a set distance. First, roll gently and see how long it takes to travel the distance. Then apply more force and compare the results.

Move it on over, pages 104–105
Objects usually move in a straight line unless another force is applied. Objects will change direction if pushed or pulled from the side. During a soccer or hockey game, balls and pucks are always changing directions as other forces are applied. Explore this idea by having children kick a rolling ball.

Stop it!, pages 106–107
Objects stop moving in their original direction when they are pushed or pulled in the opposite direction. Children could play catch to explore this idea. Ask children if they have ever caught, or been hit by, a fast-moving ball or puck. If so, they know it can hurt. The ball or puck is exerting force on the child's body. It takes more force to stop a fast-moving ball.

Down to Earth, pages 108–109
Gravity is a pulling force. Earth's gravity pulls things downwards. To explore gravity, ask children to predict what will happen when you toss a variety of objects into the air. Toss lighter or heavier objects, such as a running shoe, a crumpled paper and a coin.

Lift it!, pages 110–111
The heavier the object, the more force is needed to overcome gravity and lift it. The elastic band serves as a force meter in this activity. Have children compare lifting an empty pail and a pail full of stones or marbles. Which requires more force to lift?

Slow motion, pages 112–113
Friction is caused when one object rubs against another. Although friction slows things down, it is an important force. A certain amount of friction ensures that objects do not slide off surfaces. Have children examine different surfaces, such as those on running shoes, sleds, bicycle tires and baking sheets. Why do they think these objects have smooth or rough surfaces?

Sliding along, pages 114–115
The amount of friction varies depending on the materials that rub together. Try dragging an object over different surfaces, such as a carpet, a sidewalk or tiles. Tape or tie an elastic band to the object and observe how much the elastic stretches as the object is dragged over the different surfaces. The elastic acts as a force meter and gauges the amount of friction — the more friction the longer the elastic stretches.

Get moving!, pages 116–117
This summary explains the main principles of forces and movement.

Words to know

force: a push or a pull

friction: a force that happens when two objects rub together

gas: matter that spreads to fill the space it is in

gravity: a force that pulls objects toward Earth

liquid: matter that flows and takes the shape of the container it is in

magnetic: can be attracted by a magnet

mass: the amount of stuff in an object

material: what an object is made from

matter: any substance — solid, liquid or gas — that takes up space

part: a piece of a structure

solid: matter that holds its own shape

structure: an object made of parts joined together

texture: how something feels to the touch

Index